JOHN ADA[...]

ON THE TRANSMIGRATION OF SOULS

FOR ORCHESTRA, CHORUS, CHILDREN'S CHORUS
AND PRE-RECORDED SOUNDS

VOCAL SCORE

HENDON MUSIC

BOOSEY & HAWKES

DISTRIBUTED BY

HAL•LEONARD®
CORPORATION
7777 W. BLUEMOUND RD. P.O. BOX 13819 MILWAUKEE, WI 53213

www.boosey.com
www.halleonard.com

Published by Hendon Music, Inc.,
a Boosey & Hawkes company
35 East 21st Street
New York NY 10010

www.boosey.com

ISMN 979-051-09673-2

First printed 2009

Printed and distributed by Hal Leonard Corporation, Milwaukee WI

Co-commissioned by the New York Philharmonic and Lincoln Center's Great Performers
and made possible with the generous support of a longtime New York family

First performed on September 19, 2002 at Avery Fisher Hall, New York City,
by the New York Philharmonic, New York Choral Artists,
and Brooklyn Youth Chorus conducted by Lorin Maazel

First recorded by the New York Philharmonic, New York Choral Artists,
and Brooklyn Youth Chorus conducted by Lorin Maazel
on Nonesuch 79816-2

References to "The Unanswered Question" by Charles Ives
used by permission of Peer International Corporation

Some of the texts were drawn from missing persons signs posted by family members
around Ground Zero in the aftermath of September 11, 2001.
The composer wishes to thank Barbara Haws, archivist for the New York Philharmonic,
for providing photographs of these signs.

Texts

"Missing…"

"Remember me. Please don't ever forget me."

"It was a beautiful day."

"Missing: Jennifer de Jesus."

"Missing: Manuel Damotta."

"I see water and buildings…"

"We will miss you. We all love you. I'll miss you, my brother."

"Jeff was my uncle"

"You will never be forgotten"

"Looking for Isaias Rivera."

"Windows on the World"

"She looks so full of life in that picture."

"it feels like yesterday that I saw your beautiful face…"

"I loved him from the start."

"You will never be forgotten."

"I miss his gentleness, his intelligence, his loyalty, his love."

"Shalom"

"Remember"

The daughter says: "He was the apple of my father's eye."

The father says: "I am so full of grief. My heart is absolutely shattered."

The young man says: "…he was tall, extremely good-looking, and girls never talked to me when he was around."

The neighbor says: "She had a voice like an angel, and she shared it with everyone, in good times and bad."

The mother says: "He used to call me every day. I'm just waiting."

The lover says: "Tomorrow will be three months, yet it feels like yesterday since I saw your beautiful face, saying, 'Love you to the moon and back, forever.'"

The man's wife says: "I loved him from the start…. I wanted to dig him out. I know just where he is."

"Louis Anthony Williams. One World Trade Center. Port Authority, 66th Floor. 'We love you, Louis. Come home.'"

"Charlie Murphy. Cantor Fitzgerald. 105th Floor. Tower One North. Weight : 180 pounds. Height: 5'11". Eye color: hazel. Hair color: brown. Date of birth: July 9th, 1963. 'Please call…We love you, Chuck.'"

"My sister"

"My brother"

"My daughter"

"My son"

"Best friend to many…"

"I love you"

Instrumentation

Children's Chorus
SATB Chorus

3 Flutes (3rd doubling on Piccolo)
Piccolo
3 Oboes
2 Clarinets in B♭
Bass Clarinet in B♭
Contrabass Clarinet in B♭
2 Bassoons
Contrabassoon
4 Horns
4 Trumpets in C
3 Trombones
2 Tubas
Timpani
Percussion (4)*
2 Harps
Piano
Celesta
Quarter-tone Piano**
(may be played on Sampler)
Pre-recorded sounds
Computer-controlled sound system (optional)
Strings

Percussion 1: Glockenspiel
Percussion 2: Crotales, High Triangle
Percussion 3: Chimes, 2 High Triangles
Percussion 4: 2 High Triangles, Suspended Cymbal, Brake Drums

**Piano may be tuned ¼ step lower instead of higher. Transposed part (½ step higher) available with performance materials.

Duration: 25 minutes

Performance materials and keyboard sampler software are available from the Boosey & Hawkes Rental Library

Notes on the Sound Design

The pre-recorded soundtrack is cued to entrances in the orchestral score. Loudspeakers should surround the audience, but the playback should always be at low volume. Two versions are possible, both obtainable from the publisher:

Version 1 (recommended): six-channel surround sound. Separate sound files are operated from a laptop.

Version 2 (alternate): a two-track mix-down, played on a conventional CD player with individual cues listed as separate tracks.

ON THE TRANSMIGRATION OF SOULS

JOHN ADAMS

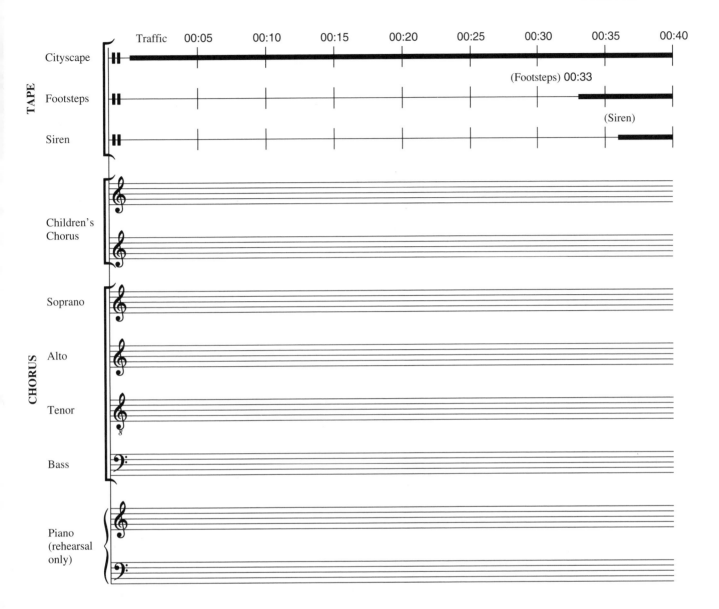

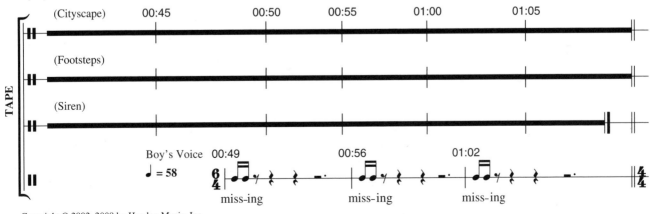

979-0-051-09673-2

Printed in U.S.A.

N.B. ū sounds like the "u" in "lure."

6

N.B. Quarter Tone Piano and Quarter Tone Ensemble
(Violins) sound one quarter tone higher than written pitch.

8

N.B. *very* subtle crescendos and diminuendos

12

14

16

18

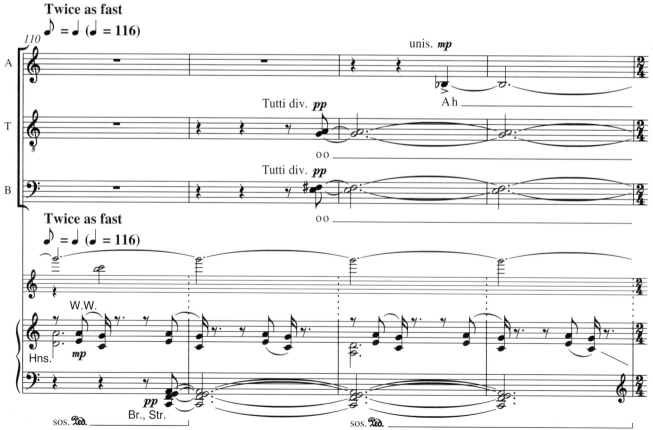

24

148

Chi.
Cho.

chain __ a-round his neck, __ a sil- ver ring, __ his mid-dle fin- ger, a small __

chain __ a-round his neck, __ a sil ver ring, __ his mid-dle fin- ger, a small __

S
div.

pp
World __

pp
World __

A

Vn.

Str.

26

(TURN PAGE SILENTLY)

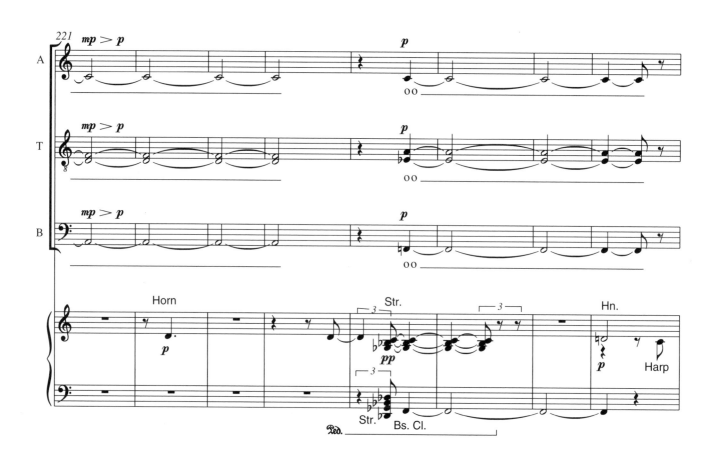

40

44

continue accel.

continue accel.

etc. through m.333

48

50

Chorus: arrange for staggered individual rests between here and m.424

52

N.B. (m.397) L.H. between 1 and 5 of R.H. (frequently through m.403)

56

58

62

(TURN PAGE SILENTLY)

64

CHORUS TACET AL FINE

Piano Reduction by Scott Eyerly